Use of English

Ten more practice tests for the **Cambridge C2 Proficiency**

Fiona Aish and Jo Tomlinson

PROSPERITY EDUCATION

PROSPERITY EDUCATION
www.prosperityeducation.net

Registered offices: Sherlock Close, Cambridge
CB3 0HP, United Kingdom

© Prosperity Education Ltd. 2021

First published 2021

ISBN: 978-1-91-382547-8

Cover design and typesetting by ORP Cambridge

For further information and resources, visit:
www.prosperityeducation.net

To infinity and beyond.

Contents

Introduction

Welcome to this second edition of sample tests for the Cambridge C2 Proficiency, Use of English (Parts 1–4).

The pass threshold of the Cambridge C2 Proficiency (CPE) examination is 60% and so, in order to allow ample time for the reading parts (Parts 5–8) of Paper 1, it is advisable that candidates complete The Use of English section (Parts 1–4) as quickly as possible while maintaining accuracy. For instance, completing each part in fewer than five minutes will allow 55 minutes in which to complete the reading parts.

This resource comprises ten whole Use of English tests, answer keys, write-in answer sheets and a marking scheme, allowing you to score each test out of 36 marks.

The content has been written to closely replicate the Cambridge exam experience, and has undergone comprehensive expert and peer review. You or your students, if you are a teacher, will hopefully enjoy the wide range of essay topics and benefit from the repetitive practice, something that is key to preparing for this part of the C2 Proficiency (CPE) examination.

We hope that you will find this resource a useful study aid, and we wish you all the best in preparing for the exam.

Fiona Aish and Jo Tomlinson
Spain, 2021

Fiona Aish and Jo Tomlinson are directors of Target English, a consultancy in Spain that provides tailor-made solutions in content creation, course provision, training and testing.

About the C2 Proficiency exam

The Use of English section of the C2 Proficiency (CPE) exam is broken down into four parts:

Part 1. Multiple choice cloze	
What is being tested?	This part of the exam mostly tests vocabulary, idioms, collocations, shades of meaning, phrasal verbs, complementation, semantic precision and fixed phrases.
How does it work?	It contains a test with eight gaps, each gap prompting multiple-choice questions. Each question has four possible answers, only one of which is correct.
How is it marked?	One mark is awarded for each correct answer.

Part 2. Open cloze	
What is being tested?	This part of the exam has a lexico-grammatical focus, testing candidates' awareness and control of grammar, fixed phrasing, collocation, semantic precision and, to an extent, vocabulary (the particles/prepositions for phrasal verbs).
How does it work?	It contains a text with eight gaps, each gap representing a missing word. No hints are given: candidates must think of the correct word for each gap.
How is it marked?	One mark is awarded for each correct answer.

Part 3. Word formation	
What is being tested?	This part of the exam focuses on affixation, internal changes and compounding in word formation, and vocabulary.
How does it work?	It contains a text with eight gaps, each gap representing a missing word. Beside each gap is a 'prompt' word that must be altered in some way to complete the sentence correctly.
How is it marked?	One mark is awarded for each correct answer.

Part 4. Key word transformations	
What is being tested?	This part of the exam has a lexico-grammatical focus, testing lexis, grammar and vocabulary.
How does it work?	It contains six sentences, each followed by a 'key' word and an alternative sentence conveying the same meaning as the first but with a gap in the middle. Candidates are to use the keyword provided to complete the second sentence so that it has a similar meaning to the first sentence. Candidates cannot change the keyword provided.
How is it marked?	Each correct answer is broken down into two marks.

Other titles for the C2 Proficiency

Visit www.prosperityeducation.net to view our wide selection of Cambridge exam resources (B2 – C2).

Reading CPE
Eight practice tests for the Cambridge C2 Proficiency

Fiona Aish and Jo Tomlinson

CPE Parts 5–7

2021

978-1913825386

100 pages

Use of English
Ten more practice tests for the Cambridge C2 Proficiency

Fiona Aish and Jo Tomlinson

CPE Parts 1–4

2021

978-1913825478

100 pages

Use of English
Ten practice tests for the Cambridge C2 Proficiency

Michael Macdonald

CPE Parts 1–4

2020

978-1916129733

100 pages

PROSPERITY EDUCATION
www.prosperityeducation.net

Cambridge
C2 Proficiency
Use of English

Test 1

For questions 1–8, read the text below and decide which answer best fits each gap. In the separate answer sheet, mark the appropriate answer (A, B, C or D).

Symphony Hall Set to Break Records

World-renowned Macklesville Symphony Hall is set for a record $15 million redevelopment amidst complaints from community groups. The existing symphony hall was constructed only twenty years ago and at a **(1)**_____ of the cost of the new proposals. However, the council has passed the new plans **(2)**_____ that the initiative to build a new hall will not only see a growth of interest in classical music and the arts in general, especially from younger audiences, but also serve as a recognition **(3)**_____ what is now the second-best orchestra in the country.

However, complaints have arisen because of a lack of **(4)**_____ regarding the plans. Local groups feel like their views have fallen on deaf ears and have even called this a **(5)**_____ misuse of public funds that cannot be justified in the current economic climate. In response, the council has insisted that a large proportion of the money for the new hall comes from private **(6)**_____, although they declined to state exact amounts. Further to this, the council sees its contribution as an investment towards the regeneration of the inner city, as well as an **(7)**_____ part of their 'Vision for Macklesville' ten-year plan. Despite these **(8)**_____, there is no stopping the plans, with building work commencing in the start of October and continuing until next spring.

1	A	fragment	B	proportion	C	fraction	D	breadth
2	A	pleading	B	implying	C	referring	D	citing
3	A	for	B	to	C	with	D	in
4	A	conjecture	B	contention	C	controversy	D	consultation
5	A	laudable	B	flagrant	C	shrouded	D	chronic
6	A	delegates	B	brokers	C	subscribers	D	donors
7	A	operative	B	indispensable	C	applicable	D	effectual
8	A	commotions	B	brawls	C	disputes	D	contrasts

For questions 9–16, read the text below and decide which word best fits each gap. Use only one word for each gap. In the separate answer sheet, write your answers in capital letters, using one box per letter.

Uncovering the Mysteries of the Tango

The tango is undeniably one of the world's most recognisable dances, evoking romantic images of graceful dancers in city squares surrounded by classical architecture. Despite having **(9)**_____ popularised in the elegant ballrooms of Paris in the early 1900s, **(10)**_____ birthplace was in the downtown streets of the 18th-century port cities of Buenos Aires and Montevideo.

One common myth about the tango's origins is that it evolved from *flamenco*, *milonga* or *habanera*, all of **(11)**_____ have their roots in Hispanic countries. However, studying sociological changes has **(12)**_____ historians to the conclusion that it is more likely to be due to the mixing of European and African cultures that went **(13)**_____ in port cities at that time, which in turn created a distinct hybrid of music and dance.

As well as its historical origins, another controversial area that stimulates a lot of heated discussions about the tango is **(14)**_____ of its symbolic meaning. Contrary to popular belief, although **(15)**_____ first glance the dancers appear to represent a loving couple, the dance actually symbolises love that is not returned. The moves communicate ideas of nostalgia, despair and tales of loss, and **(16)**_____ such the dancers perform the moves with slow, precise movements so as to transmit these feelings to the audience.

For questions 17–24, use the stem word on the right to form the correct word that fills each gap. In the separate answer sheet, write your answers in capital letters, using one box per letter.

NEW KID ON THE BLOCK

The new Bantam Sunrise is the car that everyone is talking about. A new Sport Utility Vehicle with a **(17)**_____ exterior and spacious interior, the **SENSE** Sunrise is set to take on leaders in the top-selling SUV market. But can it live up to **(18)**_____ in an **EXPECT** already overcrowded market? Our reviewers are in two minds.

This trendy SUV is geared towards the urban market, meaning that it's great for fuel efficiency, but it's far from a **(19)**_____ experience when taken off-road. **FAULT** This is all down to the fact that it is the only SUV on the market to lack a four-wheel-drive option, but this is the only surprising **(20)**_____ in its otherwise excellent **OMIT** offering.

When we take a look inside, it's clear that this car is well-built and user friendly. It doesn't feel cramped due to the clever **(21)**_____ of the cabin, which includes **COMPOSE** colour splashes to break up the interior. Best of all, it **(22)**_____ beats all other SUVs in terms of **CONCLUDE** luggage space, which often is a bone of contention in this section of the market.

This vehicle certainly does have its benefits. While it might not be suited to off-road **(23)**_____, this car has **ENTHUSE** a lot to offer the general driver. With some tweaks to later models, the Sunrise could make for an **(24)**_____ choice for those looking for a **AWE** reasonably priced SUV.

For questions 25–30, complete the second sentence, using the word given, so that it has a similar meaning to the first sentence. Do not change the word provided and use between three and eight words in total. In the separate answer sheet, write your answers in capital letters, using one box per letter.

25   You have left it very late to start looking for work.

      HIGH

      It's _____ for work.

26   The jury finally returned a guilty verdict after five days of discussion.

      WERE

      Only after five days of discussion, _____ a guilty verdict.

27   Simon couldn't take part in the tennis tournament due to the seriousness of his injury.

      HIM

      Simon's serious injury _____ in the tennis tournament.

28   You can also request a credit card with this type of account, but it is completely optional.

      APPLY

      You are _____ for a credit card with this account.

29   I would quite like to spend my holidays at home, although I know it seems dull.

      SOUNDS

      As _____, I'd quite like to spend my holidays at home.

30   In my opinion, we absolutely cannot change the wedding date now.

      QUESTION

      Changing the wedding date _____ I'm concerned.

Answer sheet: Cambridge C2 Proficiency Use of English

Test No. ☐

Mark out of 36 ☐

Name _____ **Date** _____

Part 1: Multiple choice

8 marks

Mark the appropriate answer (A, B, C or D).

| 0 | A | B | C | D |

1	A	B	C	D
2	A	B	C	D
3	A	B	C	D
4	A	B	C	D

5	A	B	C	D
6	A	B	C	D
7	A	B	C	D
8	A	B	C	D

Part 2: Open cloze

8 marks

Write your answers in capital letters, using one box per letter.

| 0 | B | E | C | A | U | S | E | | | | |

9											
10											
11											
12											
13											
14											
15											
16											

Part 3: Word formation

Write your answers in capital letters, using one box per letter.

17

18

19

20

21

22

23

24

Part 4: Key word transformation

Write your answers in capital letters, using one box per letter.

25

26

27

28

29

30

Cambridge C2 Proficiency Use of English

Test 2

For questions 1–8, read the text below and decide which answer best fits each gap. In the separate answer sheet, mark the appropriate answer (A, B, C or D).

The Benefits of Nostalgia

The other day, over coffee, my friend Angela confided her concerns about becoming overly nostalgic for her past. She'd never struck me as a **(1)**_____ person, so I was naturally concerned. I decided to mention a fascinating video I'd watched online about the subject.

Apparently, doctors used to have the misguided **(2)**_____ that nostalgia was a mental illness. However, in the last couple of decades psychologists have **(3)**_____ doubt on this. They've realised that it's actually a **(4)**_____ effective form of self-treatment in times of anxiety or isolation. In the video, a psychologist described how people derive **(5)**_____ from reliving pleasant past experiences. This is because the process releases positive chemicals in the brain that help build motivation for the future.

So, equipped with my newfound facts, I launched into the conversation hoping to make Angela feel less miserable. She started nodding enthusiastically, saying this explanation really **(6)**_____ the nail on the head. Her working environment had become quite stressful, mainly due to some issues with the company's finances, and it was really beginning to take **(7)**_____ toll on her. This was causing the nostalgic feelings, and the result was that she'd lost **(8)**_____ of the bigger picture of her life.

Anyway, she promised to watch the video herself and I hope it benefits her, too.

1	**A**	bland	**B**	sentimental	**C**	pathetic	**D**	longing
2	**A**	belief	**B**	conclusion	**C**	deduction	**D**	intuition
3	**A**	cast	**B**	dropped	**C**	thrown	**D**	shed
4	**A**	realistically	**B**	conclusively	**C**	remarkably	**D**	unanimously
5	**A**	relief	**B**	comfort	**C**	caution	**D**	freedom
6	**A**	tapped	**B**	struck	**C**	chopped	**D**	hit
7	**A**	its	**B**	some	**C**	a	**D**	all
8	**A**	standard	**B**	sight	**C**	perspective	**D**	outlook

For questions 9–16, read the text below and decide which word best fits each gap. Use only one word for each gap. In the separate answer sheet, write your answers in capital letters, using one box per letter.

A Female President?

In 2016, the USA missed out on having its first female president. However, **(9)**_____ most people don't realise is that in the early 20th century one woman single-handedly assumed the presidential role, **(10)**_____ all but name. Although never officially elected, as the wife of US President Woodrow Wilson, Edith Wilson secretly governed the entire country for over a year while her husband was seriously ill.

Upon **(11)**_____, it was love at first sight between Edith and Woodrow, and she soon became one of his trusted advisors, despite having no political experience, a development with which Wilson's administrative team were ill at **(12)**_____ to say the least. Despite objections, Edith and Woodrow soon married and she became engaged **(13)**_____ helping the President with his work, unofficially, with full access to all kinds of classified materials.

When Woodrow had a stroke, Edith would not contemplate that he should resign from the role as President and have the Vice President step in. She decided instead to cover **(14)**_____ his illness by taking on his duties in secret. According to her and her personal physicians, Woodrow was working from his bedroom, and she insisted that all presidential work come **(15)**_____ her, even firing staff members who disobeyed. Many at the time claimed it was clear to see the lack of governance, but all things considered, for a working-class girl who had to **(16)**_____ it by ear, she didn't do a bad job.

For questions 17–24, use the stem word on the right to form the correct word that fills each gap. In the separate answer sheet, write your answers in capital letters, using one box per letter.

Job Interview Advice

Nerves affect even the most confident person before a job interview, which is why preparation and attitude are vital. Being chosen for an interview means that, on paper, you have all the necessary **(17)**_____. So, when **QUALIFY**

preparing remember that you are **(18)**_____ **WORTH** of the interviewer's time. However, so are the rest of the interviewees, which means you need stand out.

While you have fulfilled the essential criteria on the job specification, look at the list of **(19)**_____ **DESIRE** attributes closely. Focusing on these will **(20)**_____ your thinking in preparation for the **SHARP** interview.

Background research on the organisation prior to your interview will be helpful, too, as it will enable you to better **(21)**_____ to the interviewer. This helps to **RELATIONSHIP** understand the type of person they want to fit the organisational culture. Another characteristic to highlight is that of being **(22)**_____ as it is a highly valued **RESOURCE** trait nowadays. Just remember that you'll need concrete examples.

Lastly, is your approach on the day. From your initial step inside the building present a picture of **(23)**_____ to everyone you encounter, from **CHEER** the reception staff to senior management. Even though you may be nervous, whatever happens in the interview will be a learning curve. Try to convince yourself that this could be a **(24)**_____ experience. You never **PLEASURE** know, you might just get the job!

For questions 25–30, complete the second sentence, using the word given, so that it has a similar meaning to the first sentence. Do not change the word provided and use between three and eight words in total. In the separate answer sheet, write your answers in capital letters, using one box per letter.

25   The director was surprised, as there wasn't any indication that he'd be the winner.

WHATSOEVER

There was _____ the director would win the award.

26   Joyce had a difficult life as a child and so joined the army at a young age.

CONTEND

Joyce joined the army so young, because she had a _____ growing up.

27   I love oysters, but I know they are not to everyone's taste.

NOSES

A lot of people _____, but I think they're delicious.

28   The bakery continues to be successful despite the new supermarket in town.

STRONG

Even though there is a new supermarket in town, the bakery _____.

29   Peter had spent so much time practising that there was no doubt he'd pass his driving test.

BOUND

By the amount of practice he's done, Peter _____ his driving test.

30   We haven't confirmed the reports yet, so would you mind waiting before you make any announcements?

HOLD

Could _____ announcements until we can confirm the reports?

Answer sheet: Cambridge C2 Proficiency
Use of English

Mark out of 36

Name _____   **Date** _____

Part 1: Multiple choice   8 marks

Mark the appropriate answer (A, B, C or D).

0	A	B	C	D

1	A	B	C	D		5	A	B	C	D
2	A	B	C	D		6	A	B	C	D
3	A	B	C	D		7	A	B	C	D
4	A	B	C	D		8	A	B	C	D

Part 2: Open cloze   8 marks

Write your answers in capital letters, using one box per letter.

0	B	E	C	A	U	S	E				

9											
10											
11											
12											
13											
14											
15											
16											

Part 3: Word formation

8 marks

Write your answers in capital letters, using one box per letter.

17
18
19
20
21
22
23
24

Part 4: Key word transformation

12 marks

Write your answers in capital letters, using one box per letter.

25

26

27

28

29

30

Cambridge C2 Proficiency Use of English

Test 3

For questions 1–8, read the text below and decide which answer best fits each gap. In the separate answer sheet, mark the appropriate answer (A, B, C or D).

The Real Count of Monte Cristo?

Many people are familiar with the classic Alexander Dumas novel, *The Count of Monte Cristo*. The book tells the story of a man who escapes after being falsely imprisoned and **(1)**_____ his sights on taking revenge on those who wronged him. However, there has been much debate on whether the tale was purely a work of fiction or whether it had some **(2)**_____ of truth to it. Some claim it was French geologist Déodat de Dolomieu, a cellmate of Dumas' father for a brief period, who **(3)**_____ rise to the famous tale of revenge.

However, a far more convincing candidate for Dumas' inspiration is a French shoemaker, Pierre Picaud, who was wrongfully accused of being a spy by three of his friends, and, as a result, was **(4)**_____ and sentenced to seven years in jail. After serving his time and receiving the inheritance of a fellow prisoner in a neighbouring cell, Picaud returned to France under a false name and with great riches, bearing little resemblance to the **(5)**_____ shoemaker he once was. He took the law **(6)**_____ his own hands in order to get revenge on his three friends, one of **(7)**_____ had married Picaud's fiancé. He **(8)**_____ his old so-called friends and successfully exacted his revenge on all three, not unlike the plot of Dumas' novel. While the story seems incredible, it is truly evident that truth is stranger than fiction.

1	**A**	takes	**B**	sets	**C**	trains	**D**	poses
2	**A**	suspicion	**B**	component	**C**	wedge	**D**	element
3	**A**	gave	**B**	took	**C**	brought	**D**	offered
4	**A**	condemned	**B**	testified	**C**	pleaded	**D**	convicted
5	**A**	scruffy	**B**	humble	**C**	mediocre	**D**	quaint
6	**A**	upon	**B**	before	**C**	into	**D**	by
7	**A**	which	**B**	who	**C**	them	**D**	whom
8	**A**	tracked down	**B**	clung to	**C**	tipped off	**D**	went by

For questions 9–16, read the text below and decide which word best fits each gap. Use only one word for each gap. In the separate answer sheet, write your answers in capital letters, using one box per letter.

Humour across cultures

Humour is a uniquely human quality that enables people to connect, break boundaries and share common ideas. However, **(9)**_____ many know through bitter experience, it does not always translate well across cultures. This is because much of **(10)**_____ we find amusing is culturally determined.

The norms of humour that are familiar to the people of one nation can seem impenetrable to **(11)**_____. However, research shows that universal elements do exist. These can cross cultural boundaries and tap into a mutual understanding of the world, irrespective **(12)**_____ where we grew up.

While many people think being funny requires **(13)**_____ certain sophistication or intellectual ability, apparently anyone can make others laugh. This is due to the fact that human beings are naturally predisposed to humour. Researchers have discovered that something commonly considered to be funny is composed of two elements. Firstly, **(14)**_____ must subvert the listener's expectations – in other words, be surprising – and, also, it must not be threatening. As this appears to hold true across cultures, the topics are where the differences lie. For example, in some countries people enjoy telling jokes about **(15)**_____ competitive relationships with neighbouring nations while, in other parts of the world people like comedy that is directed at themselves, or like using wordplay, storytelling or satire.

Whatever the topic, though, it turns out that understanding the things that make any of us crack **(16)**_____ isn't actually that difficult.

For questions 17–24, use the stem word on the right to form the correct word that fills each gap. In the separate answer sheet, write your answers in capital letters, using one box per letter.

A Morning Essential?

Coffee is probably one of the most popular drinks in the world, especially in the mornings when people need something to perk them up and assist them with getting on with their days. For many of us, it would simply be **(17)**_____ to start the day without at least one cup of roasting-hot coffee, but do we really need it?   **CONCEIVE**

Obviously, **(18)**_____ coffee addicts will tell you that a hit of caffeine is not only pleasant, but an essential part of their morning routine, largely because people believe that it is coffee that makes them **(19)**_____, fully functioning members of society.   **CURE**

INDUSTRY

However, the health effects of coffee are controversial, which is why an increasing number of people are turning to **(20)**_____ versions, or even drinks such as green tea. Coffee can have negative consequences for people who are prone to anxiety or restlessness, and it also becomes a habit that is hard to break. People who drink coffee regularly find it literally **(21)**_____, and stopping can lead to withdrawal symptoms.   **CAFFEINE**

RESIST

Perhaps this **(22)**_____ is also a reason why people are turning to alternatives. Nobody wants to be addicted to something, albeit **(23)**_____. This interest in alternative choice is, of course, a good idea, but although coffee is occasionally disparaged by the press and health professionals alike, it also has some clearly beneficial **(24)**_____. Studies have shown that coffee can help protect people from numerous illnesses, such as diabetes and Alzheimer's.   **REALISE**

CONCIOUS

CHARACTER

For questions 25–30, complete the second sentence, using the word given, so that it has a similar meaning to the first sentence. Do not change the word provided and use between three and eight words in total. In the separate answer sheet, write your answers in capital letters, using one box per letter.

25   Elena had a nose operation because she didn't like the way it looked.

      IT

      Elena didn't like the look of her nose so she _____.

26   You wouldn't have to ask me twice to appear on TV.

      JUMP

      I _____ on TV.

27   Don't you even think about leaving your rubbish on the street.

      BETTER

      You _____ your rubbish in the street.

28   Social media is flooded with people trying to become well-known for something or other.

      NAME

      There is a multitude of people trying _____ themselves on social media.

29   Jorge was late for the bus, so he had no choice but to run.

      MAKE

      Jorge _____ to catch the bus on time.

30   The decorators were here from early morning until the evening, just to paint the living room.

      BEST

      It took the decorators _____ just to paint the living room.

Answer sheet: Cambridge C2 Proficiency
Use of English

Test No. ☐

Mark out of 36 ☐

Name _____   **Date** _____

Part 1: Multiple choice

8 marks

Mark the appropriate answer (A, B, C or D).

0	A	**B**	C	D	

1	A	B	C	D			5	A	B	C	D
2	A	B	C	D			6	A	B	C	D
3	A	B	C	D			7	A	B	C	D
4	A	B	C	D			8	A	B	C	D

Part 2: Open cloze

8 marks

Write your answers in capital letters, using one box per letter.

0	B	E	C	A	U	S	E				

9											
10											
11											
12											
13											
14											
15											
16											

Part 3: Word formation

8 marks

Write your answers in capital letters, using one box per letter.

17

18

19

20

21

22

23

24

Part 4: Key word transformation

12 marks

Write your answers in capital letters, using one box per letter.

25

26

27

28

29

30

Cambridge C2 Proficiency Use of English

Test 4

For questions 1–8, read the text below and decide which answer best fits each gap. In the separate answer sheet, mark the appropriate answer (A, B, C or D).

Thailand's floating markets

For those of you yet to experience the wonders of the floating markets of Thailand, I can tell you that you're in for a spectacular **(1)**_____. Visits to these markets are made on a traditional narrow boat and, as you approach, your senses will be overwhelmed. The sights, sounds and smells are amazing, and a **(2)**_____ display of produce is on offer.

Floating markets were originally constructed as a means to an **(3)**_____. This was so that traders, keen to avoid the bustling streets of Bangkok, could easily transport their goods on the city's waterways. Before long, these slender canals expanded to other cities around the country. Nowadays, these colourful markets attract vast quantities of tourists and are a **(4)**_____ element of local economies.

Getting the most out of your market trip involves real commitment. The Damnoen Saduak market, for instance, gets very crowded, so **(5)**_____ an early start and aim to arrive no later than 7am. Booking an organised tour is the most convenient thing to do, but bear **(6)**_____ mind that you should factor in travelling time of about an hour. This could mean getting up at dawn. Also, tourists are expected to make at least one purchase while at the market. This doesn't necessarily mean **(7)**_____ out on expensive produce, but these markets are how many people earn a living, so act like a responsible tourist and make a point **(8)**_____ buying something.

1	**A**	satisfaction	**B**	comfort	**C**	treat	**D**	relief
2	**A**	profound	**B**	quaint	**C**	dazzling	**D**	muddled
3	**A**	end	**B**	action	**C**	odds	**D**	use
4	**A**	paramount	**B**	structural	**C**	supporting	**D**	fundamental
5	**A**	do	**B**	make	**C**	have	**D**	take
6	**A**	in	**B**	on	**C**	at	**D**	to
7	**A**	splashing	**B**	struggling	**C**	succumbing	**D**	straining
8	**A**	for	**B**	of	**C**	from	**D**	over

For questions 9–16, read the text below and decide which word best fits each gap. Use only one word for each gap. In the separate answer sheet, write your answers in capital letters, using one box per letter.

The history of writing

Writing is a medium of communication that most people use daily, and perhaps even take for granted. Yet, without a shadow of a **(9)**_____, it has been one of the key elements in the development of society. Writing systems and the invention of books have meant that knowledge can be passed on reliably through the generations.

Much evidence suggests that **(10)**_____ was in the Middle East that systems of writing were initially developed, and these were borne out of practical necessity. As individuals grouped together in cities, this **(11)**_____ rise to more frequent trading of goods, but keeping a running order of these goods was an **(12)**_____ battle, especially since they were often communally stored.

(13)_____ the face of these difficulties, a better method of controlling and accounting **(14)**_____ stock was developed, and this was the very first system of writing. It initially took the form of pictures drawn in clay tablets to represent a particular commodity, with lines corresponding to the number of items a person had. In time, these drawings gave **(15)**_____ to symbols, which were more efficient for the writer, and then to more detailed forms of written record. This is when writing evolved to more than just lists of nouns, and started to **(16)**_____ the shape of the fully formed sentences we see today.

For questions 17–24, use the stem word on the right to form the correct word that fills each gap. In the separate answer sheet, write your answers in capital letters, using one box per letter.

Success in business and sport

The careers of business leaders and professional athletes have much in common, even though they can appear to be very different. For one thing, both groups are concerned with the **(17)**_____ of success in **PURSUE** their chosen fields. Whether they are professional players on the tennis court or CEOs in a tough meeting, the same **(18)**_____ determination is present. In **CHARACTER** addition, both groups employ the services of others to help them achieve their goals. Everyone knows that sportspeople are under the direction of a trainer or manager. However, for many business leaders there is a strong **(19)**_____ that they have hired a life **LIKE** coach or personal **(20)**_____ for support. **CONSULT**

It's interesting to look at these people in more detail.

For both groups, the overall **(21)**_____ of their **ESSENTIAL** approach is a commitment to improving their performance. While it may seem obvious that sportspeople are able to resist pizza and lying around on the sofa, business leaders also create lifestyles that are **(22)**_____ directed towards opportunities for **STRATEGY** success.

Examining the mindset of both groups can help us to understand from where this personality type might **(23)**_____. It has been suggested that this **ORIGIN** single-minded attitude might come from a need for control and a desire to avoid the many **(24)**_____ in **AMBIGUOUS** life. In this way, athletes and business leaders can stay focused instead of getting distracted like everyone else.

For questions 25–30, complete the second sentence, using the word given, so that it has a similar meaning to the first sentence. Do not change the word provided and use between three and eight words in total. In the separate answer sheet, write your answers in capital letters, using one box per letter.

25   Helena was about to leave work when the email came in.

      VERGE

      The email arrived just as Helena _____ work.

26   The video quality will deteriorate if you want to reduce the file size.

      EXPENSE

      The file size can be reduced, but it _____ the video
      quality.

27   The manager said that he couldn't do anything, despite the man's complaint
      about his faulty television.

      DONE

      He complained to the manager who said that _____
      the faulty television.

28   Eva and Javi didn't like each other at first, but now they are great friends.

      WRONG

      Eva and Javi are great friends, even though they _____.

29   They missed the start of the film because they had taken too long getting to the
      cinema.

      MOVE

      If they _____ on, they would have seen the start of
      the film.

30   You can't go home until everybody has finished their writing.

      ONLY

      _____ their writing can you go home.

Answer sheet: Cambridge C2 Proficiency
Use of English

Test No. ☐

Mark out of 36 ☐

Name _____ **Date** _____

Part 1: Multiple choice   8 marks

Mark the appropriate answer (A, B, C or D).

| 0 | A | **B** | C | D | |

1	A	B	C	D			5	A	B	C	D	
2	A	B	C	D			6	A	B	C	D	
3	A	B	C	D			7	A	B	C	D	
4	A	B	C	D			8	A	B	C	D	

Part 2: Open cloze   8 marks

Write your answers in capital letters, using one box per letter.

| 0 | B | E | C | A | U | S | E | | | | |

9										
10										
11										
12										
13										
14										
15										
16										

Part 3: Word formation

Write your answers in capital letters, using one box per letter.

17

18

19

20

21

22

23

24

Part 4: Key word transformation

Write your answers in capital letters, using one box per letter.

25

26

27

28

29

30

PROSPERITY EDUCATION
www.prosperityeducation.net

Cambridge
C2 Proficiency
Use of English

Test 5

For questions 1–8, read the text below and decide which answer best fits each gap. In the separate answer sheet, mark the appropriate answer (A, B, C or D).

Too hot to handle

"The spicier the better," a friend of mine boasted before he **(1)**_____ sweat through the inferno of a curry before him, drinking copious amounts of water to, doubtlessly, numb the pain. We were out for a **(2)**_____ to eat at a local Indian restaurant, where, for some bewildering reason, a ritual of 'manliness' has arisen amongst my **(3)**_____ of friends. That is, the amount of spice that you can withstand is directly connected to the amount of manliness you embody.

To be quite frank, I wasn't **(4)**_____ with any tolerance of spice. Even the most mildly spiced foods get me coughing and spluttering, and desperately reaching for my water. I'd always taken this kind of boasting with a pinch of salt, assuming that the ability to handle spice is **(5)**_____ and that I was powerless to counteract it. Yet, apparently, a tolerance to spice is something that can be learned. This is why many people from India and Mexico seem to be able to consume much spicier foods than those from, say, Scotland can. It's simply **(6)**_____ to the fact that chilies are an integral part of their diet since childhood, hence they become desensitised to the heat. Unfortunately for me, there was a profound lack of them in my Scottish diet growing up.

In **(7)**_____, I like to be able to taste all the flavours in my food, not just experience a burning sensation, so I suppose I had better **(8)**_____ myself out of any more macho competitions!

1	**A**	battled from	**B**	proceeded to	**C**	advanced through	**D**	suffered with
2	**A**	mouth	**B**	fare	**C**	meal	**D**	bite
3	**A**	circle	**B**	turn	**C**	crew	**D**	square
4	**A**	endowed	**B**	constrained	**C**	embodied	**D**	replenished
5	**A**	receptive	**B**	immune	**C**	innate	**D**	eccentric
6	**A**	up	**B**	down	**C**	round	**D**	over
7	**A**	retrospect	**B**	the clear	**C**	good taste	**D**	all honesty
8	**A**	cast	**B**	number	**C**	rule	**D**	figure

For questions 9–16, read the text below and decide which word best fits each gap. Use only one word for each gap. In the separate answer sheet, write your answers in capital letters, using one box per letter.

A Famous Language Myth

The myth that the languages of the Inuit peoples of the Arctic contain hundreds of words for snow has continued long after **(9)**_____ was disproved. This is somewhat of a mystery. At some level it could have been a bad joke that **(10)**_____ out of hand, and was popularised because it sounded plausible. Yet, it also demonstrates that, until recently, very **(11)**_____ was understood about many of the world's languages.

The snow myth started in the 1940s. The controversial linguist Benjamin Whorf claimed that the Inuit perceived snow differently and therefore required a far wider vocabulary **(12)**_____ which to describe it. Over the following decades the myth snowballed **(13)**_____ his initial assumption of just seven alternative words. Not long after, newspapers and textbooks alike were reporting the number as upwards **(14)**_____ a hundred.

What these early linguists failed to understand was the construction of the Inuit languages. In creating complex descriptive words, additional units are added to the root word **(15)**_____ opposed to English where separate words perform this function. So, while English would use two words, such as 'melting ice', an Inuit language would combine them to form one word, e.g. 'meltingice'.

Attempting to assign **(16)**_____ finite number of words for anything in these languages is therefore meaningless since the possibilities are potentially infinite. However, like countless myths in popular culture, this one has also proved hard to kill!

For questions 17–24, use the stem word on the right to form the correct word that fills each gap. In the separate answer sheet, write your answers in capital letters, using one box per letter.

Extract from a novel: *The Debt*

It was at that point I knew I must attempt to make it back home and stop the terrible fate awaiting my wife. As I battled through the blustering snow to my car, I feared I'd be too late. Conditions were **(17)**_____, and I had no choice but to crawl along to my destination at a paralysing speed.

HAZARD

I had **(18)**_____ become mixed up with the wrong people, looking for a quick fix to my debt problems and now my wife was going to pay. It was madness to think I could get entangled with the Bartletts and walk away **(19)**_____, but I never thought they'd go after my family, and now the most **(20)**_____ member of the clan, Sam Bartlett, was somewhere close to home.

SENSE

AFFECT

MERCY

I was ploughing my way ahead on the deserted forest highway, with the **(21)**_____ of her fate playing on my every thought, when suddenly I spotted a car blocking the road ahead, broken down, undoubtedly, and ditched, possibly. I slowed to a stop, in the despairing realisation that this could delay me **(22)**_____.

CERTAIN

DEFINITE

I wrestled against the wind on foot to get to the car, and had bent down to the driver's window when I was dumbstruck by the **(23)**_____ vision of my wife at the wheel. What was she doing there, on this deserted road, in a car that was **(24)**_____ to me? I looked at her questioningly, as she mouthed slowly: "Bartlett is in the back."

EXPLAIN

RECOGNISE

For questions 25–30, complete the second sentence, using the word given, so that it has a similar meaning to the first sentence. Do not change the word provided and use between three and eight words in total. In the separate answer sheet, write your answers in capital letters, using one box per letter.

25   Although our scheduled landing time is 07.05, we'll be landing fifteen minutes earlier.

   DUE

   The plane _____ of schedule.

26   Tony doesn't like people who ask to borrow money.

   KINDLY

   Tony _____ who ask to borrow money.

27   A mobile phone started ringing just as the film had started.

   HAD

   Hardly _____ when a mobile phone started ringing.

28   The actress found the newspaper article offensive, and rightly so!

   EXCEPTION

   The actress had every right _____ newspaper article.

29   Most shop assistants aren't in the least bothered by rude customers.

   WATER

   Rude customers are _____ to the majority of shop assistants.

30   Debbie always tried to help somebody in need.

   BACK

   Debbie would never _____ needed her.

Part 1: Multiple choice

8 marks

Mark the appropriate answer (A, B, C or D).

0	A	B	C	D

1	A	B	C	D

2	A	B	C	D

3	A	B	C	D

4	A	B	C	D

5	A	B	C	D

6	A	B	C	D

7	A	B	C	D

8	A	B	C	D

Part 2: Open cloze

8 marks

Write your answers in capital letters, using one box per letter.

| 0 | B | E | C | A | U | S | E | | | | |

9										
10										
11										
12										
13										
14										
15										
16										

Part 3: Word formation

Write your answers in capital letters, using one box per letter.

17 | | | | | | | | | | |

18 | | | | | | | | | | |

19 | | | | | | | | | | |

20 | | | | | | | | | | |

21 | | | | | | | | | | |

22 | | | | | | | | | | |

23 | | | | | | | | | | |

24 | | | | | | | | | | |

Part 4: Key word transformation

12 marks

Write your answers in capital letters, using one box per letter.

25 | | | | | | | | | | | | | | | | | | | | |

26 | | | | | | | | | | | | | | | | | | | | |

27 | | | | | | | | | | | | | | | | | | | | |

28 | | | | | | | | | | | | | | | | | | | | |

29 | | | | | | | | | | | | | | | | | | | | |

30 | | | | | | | | | | | | | | | | | | | | |

Cambridge
C2 Proficiency
Use of English

Test 6

For questions 1–8, read the text below and decide which answer best fits each gap. In the separate answer sheet, mark the appropriate answer (A, B, C or D).

Texting while driving: latest update

The local police are aiming to crack **(1)**_____ on mobile phone use in cars after twenty accidents this year have happened as a result of texting and calling while driving. Until last year, **(2)**_____ was vague and the police have been **(3)**_____ towards drivers who ignore the rules. Yet, after such a considerable rise in accidents that demonstrate a clear connection to careless driving, police are now determined to take action. Anyone caught using their mobile phone will have **(4)**_____ pressed against them, irrespective of the circumstances.

This comes **(5)**_____ complaints from local residents about dangerous driving, especially since the recent introduction of the new one-way system through the city centre. The system was designed to **(6)**_____ congestion. However, at a recent council meeting with representatives from local residents' groups in attendance, people claimed that, despite the reduction in traffic jams, the Widmark Road area has become an accident black spot. They said that the new measures have seen a rise in complacency in drivers, hence the mobile phone use.

These residents' groups have put the blame **(7)**_____ on the council and have requested urgent changes. They claim that, up until now the council and local police have **(8)**_____ their backs on the problems, preferring instead to address less important issues such as parking fines. Let's hope the crackdown makes a difference.

1	A	down	B	on	C	against	D	for
2	A	ruling	B	instruction	C	formation	D	legislation
3	A	lenient	B	unwilling	C	useless	D	appreciative
4	A	complaints	B	forces	C	charges	D	laws
5	A	prior to	B	amid	C	throughout	D	along
6	A	handle	B	erode	C	favour	D	ease
7	A	profoundly	B	squarely	C	invariably	D	merely
8	A	turned	B	given	C	put	D	set

For questions 9–16, read the text below and decide which word best fits each gap. Use only one word for each gap. In the separate answer sheet, write your answers in capital letters, using one box per letter.

A Medical Marvel

There couldn't be a more unfortunate time to be struck **(9)**_____ by some mystery illness than when you're in some remote outpost, hundreds of miles from medical assistance, but this was a common occurrence in the early-1900s Australian outback. **(10)**_____ such example is the case of Jimmy Darcy, a farmer on a remote smallholding who needed urgent medical attention. After travelling around 12 hours to get to the nearest civilization, a post office, he then had to be operated on by the post office worker, while medical assistance was on its **(11)**_____. This was in the form of a doctor, who travelled first by boat, then car, then horse-drawn cart and, finally, on foot to arrive ten days later, and sadly two days too late to help Jimmy, who by then had succumbed **(12)**_____ his illness.

It was such tragedies as **(13)**_____ that inspired the Flying Doctor Service in Australia. At the time, long-distance medical aid seemed **(14)**_____ of the question, but just as the need became more apparent, the technology became available to help. Small aircraft and radio technology **(15)**_____ into play to provide medical attention to those in more remote areas via the use of pedal radios that were given to stations around Australia, and planes which flew from a central command. Incredibly, all of this was made possible through the donations and fundraising of individuals and, not long after, the service **(16)**_____ become the world's first official air ambulance.

For questions 17–24, use the stem word on the right to form the correct word that fills each gap. In the separate answer sheet, write your answers in capital letters, using one box per letter.

What is inspiration?

Inspiration is often seen as being synonymous with creativity and spontaneity. We believe that it appears out of nowhere and that being truly inspirational is **(17)**_____ for most of us. It seems that **ATTAIN** inspiring creatives, revered in society, are artists and designers not marking managers, or teachers.

However, this **(18)**_____ couldn't be further **PERCEIVE** from the truth. In all walks of life, inspiration comes from modifying existing ideas and plenty of inventions **(19)**_____ this. Roll-on deodorant is a case in **EXAMPLE** point where its inventor used the same design principles as the ball-point pen. This highlights how easily people **(20)**_____ this concept of inspiration. They **INTERPRETATION** see it as some kind of genius trick when it is no such thing. Another error in our thinking is that inspiration must in some way be **(21)**_____. People think that **INTELLECT** it emerges from a well-rounded knowledge of the arts and culture. Again, this is an illusion; inspiration can be triggered by a potentially limitless range of ideas or experiences.

So, for those wondering how to pinpoint your particular **(22)**_____, start monitoring what takes your **STIMULATE** attention on a daily basis and certain things will soon become obvious. To capitalise on this, being **(23)**_____ in creating the conditions in which **PERSIST** your inspiration can surface is important. Inspirational people **(24)**_____ embrace and work with the **READY** ideas of others rather than waiting endlessly for their personal 'light bulb moment'.

For questions 25–30, complete the second sentence, using the word given, so that it has a similar meaning to the first sentence. Do not change the word provided and use between three and eight words in total. In the separate answer sheet, write your answers in capital letters, using one box per letter.

25 Ian had to buy his wife a present, but he was at a loss as to what to get her.

IDEA

Ian didn't have the _____ to get his wife as a present.

26 United's loss against Newcastle could only be described as a disaster.

SHORT

United's loss against Newcastle _____ disaster.

27 They were completely ignorant that their lottery ticket had won.

KNOW

Little _____ won the lottery.

28 You could always count on Steve to have a great idea at meetings.

SLEEVE

Steve always _____ at meetings.

29 As long as he stayed out of trouble, he was free to go.

CONDITION

He was released _____ make any more trouble.

30 They didn't believe him until they'd questioned him for hours.

SUBJECTED

They _____ before they believed him.

Answer sheet: Cambridge C2 Proficiency
Use of English

Test No.

Mark out of 36

Name _____ **Date** _____

Part 1: Multiple choice

8 marks

Mark the appropriate answer (A, B, C or D).

0	A	B	C	D

1	A	B	C	D		5	A	B	C	D
2	A	B	C	D		6	A	B	C	D
3	A	B	C	D		7	A	B	C	D
4	A	B	C	D		8	A	B	C	D

Part 2: Open cloze

8 marks

Write your answers in capital letters, using one box per letter.

0	B	E	C	A	U	S	E				

9											
10											
11											
12											
13											
14											
15											
16											

Part 3: Word formation

Write your answers in capital letters, using one box per letter.

17

18

19

20

21

22

23

24

Part 4: Key word transformation

Write your answers in capital letters, using one box per letter.

25

26

27

28

29

30

Cambridge C2 Proficiency Use of English

Test 7

Making a habit stick

If only we had a penny for every time we've heard someone declare, "I've started a new exercise **(1)**_____," or "I'm cutting out junk food," only to **(2)**_____ in the towel within weeks, we'd probably be millionaires! But, in all honestly, forming a new habit is no mean **(3)**_____, in spite of the fact that our entire lives are permeated by daily habits. However, many scientists assert that the reason our efforts to change are often in vain is simply because we're going about it all wrong.

According to the experts, the most effective way to embark on a new habit, and stick to it, is to **(4)**_____ it into existing routines, and in small steps rather than sweeping changes. If you set unrealistic expectations, then you won't, in all **(5)**_____, sustain them. So, for example, don't set about training for a marathon if you generally have trouble peeling yourself off the sofa. Your best bet is to take **(6)**_____ steps, like doing some walking on-the-spot while waiting for the kettle to boil for your morning tea – and this has the additional benefit of fitting in with an already formed habit – tea drinking! This will make it easier for you to be **(7)**_____, which is the key to forming habits, as automation will take the place of willpower, and you'll simply start going through **(8)**_____ of your new habit subconsciously.

1	**A**	reign	**B**	regime	**C**	drill	**D**	mandate
2	**A**	relax	**B**	chip	**C**	throw	**D**	give
3	**A**	deed	**B**	feat	**C**	coup	**D**	quest
4	**A**	incorporate	**B**	initiate	**C**	infiltrate	**D**	imitate
5	**A**	confidence	**B**	perspective	**C**	retrospect	**D**	probability
6	**A**	discernible	**B**	favourable	**C**	incremental	**D**	arbitrary
7	**A**	consistent	**B**	perpetual	**C**	ardent	**D**	persistent
8	**A**	the roof	**B**	the motions	**C**	the waves	**D**	the flow

For questions 9–16, read the text below and decide which word best fits each gap. Use only one word for each gap. In the separate answer sheet, write your answers in capital letters, using one box per letter.

Where would we be without the shipping container?

Few of us ever pause for a moment to think about how all the goods we consume appear in stores and markets the world over **(9)**_____ such regularity week in week out. This smooth-running global transportation network results from **(10)**_____ appears to be a rather mundane innovation – the shipping container. However, the transformational effects of this steel box ought not to be underestimated.

Before uniformly shaped containers could be mechanically loaded on top of each other, **(11)**_____ obviously efficient system existed. Boxes were unloaded by hand, which was an extremely laborious process for all concerned. Besides this time-consuming process, companies faced the additional expenditure of warehouse storage on **(12)**_____ of the poor durability of boxes that were frequently destroyed by adverse weather.

The initial shipping container design can be attributed **(13)**_____ Malcolm McLean. He was the owner of a trucking company in 1950s America. Experience had taught him that **(14)**_____ so many consumer goods could be transported over land. As a result, he wanted to experiment with making sea transportation more financially viable. He **(15)**_____ the plunge, borrowed a considerable sum of money and started sketching his ideas.

His attempts resulted in a stackable, strong container that reduced loading costs by up to 90%. Since then, international trade has exploded and shows no signs of slowing down. McLean would likely be astonished by the impact his invention has **(16)**_____ on the world economy.

For questions 17–24, use the stem word on the right to form the correct word that fills each gap. In the separate answer sheet, write your answers in capital letters, using one box per letter.

Politician Innocent

After a six-month government inquiry, Douglas Jones, the Member of Parliament for Salesford, has been found innocent of all claims of misuse of public funds. The inquiry focused on allegations that Mr Jones had **(17)**_____ claimed a substantial amount for **REPORT** expenses for services and goods that in fact his family and friends were the recipients of rather than Mr Jones himself. These expenses and goods included international travel and entertainment equipment, and amounted to a **(18)**_____ value of around two hundred **MONEY** thousand pounds.

Claims released in the press led to a **(19)**_____ in the government chamber, with **CONFRONT** members of other parties calling his spending behaviour **(20)**_____ at best, with many others calling **RATION** for him to be investigated over illegal activity. At the time Jones claimed his spending was **(21)**_____, **JUSTIFY** as members of his social circle and family worked in his office as support staff.

While the inquiry stated Jones' innocence of any criminal wrongdoing, it also judged that he had been **(22)**_____ in the manner by which he had **THINK** accounted for his expenses, and indicated that he needed to be able to **(23)**_____ more clearly between **DIFFER** his personal expenses and government expenses. Jones remains **(24)**_____, stating that all his **APOLOGY** spending is correct and in order, yet has guaranteed to overhaul his accounting procedures to ensure no such allegations reoccur.

For questions 25–30, complete the second sentence, using the word given, so that it has a similar meaning to the first sentence. Do not change the word provided and use between three and eight words in total. In the separate answer sheet, write your answers in capital letters, using one box per letter.

25   People had a far stronger belief in politicians in the past.

LIKELY

Politicians were _____ believed in the past.

26   Setting up a successful business involves working more than most people do.

GO

In order to _____ a new business, it's essential to work overtime.

27   Eventually we decided to move because the garden was too small for our needs.

BEEN

We would have stayed in that house _____ the size of the garden.

28   My father is a government employee so they can send him to work in different places.

POSTED

Working for the government means that my father _____ anywhere in the country.

29   I can see Harry ending up with burnout soon if he carries on working as much as this.

RUNNING

Working so hard means that _____ becoming burnt out soon.

30   Oscar changed his mind about staying in the hotel after he noticed how much it cost.

HEART

Although Oscar was initially keen on the hotel, he had _____ upon seeing the room rates.

Answer sheet: Cambridge C2 Proficiency
Use of English

Test No. ☐

Mark out of 36 ☐

Name _____ **Date** _____

Part 1: Multiple choice

8 marks

Mark the appropriate answer (A, B, C or D).

0	A	B	C	D

1	A	B	C	D		5	A	B	C	D
2	A	B	C	D		6	A	B	C	D
3	A	B	C	D		7	A	B	C	D
4	A	B	C	D		8	A	B	C	D

Part 2: Open cloze

8 marks

Write your answers in capital letters, using one box per letter.

0	B	E	C	A	U	S	E				

9											
10											
11											
12											
13											
14											
15											
16											

Part 3: Word formation

8 marks

Write your answers in capital letters, using one box per letter.

17 □□□□□□□□□□□

18 □□□□□□□□□□□

19 □□□□□□□□□□□

20 □□□□□□□□□□□

21 □□□□□□□□□□□

22 □□□□□□□□□□□

23 □□□□□□□□□□□

24 □□□□□□□□□□□

Part 4: Key word transformation

12 marks

Write your answers in capital letters, using one box per letter.

25 □□□□□□□□□□□□□□□□□□□
□□□□□□□□□□□□□□□□□□

26 □□□□□□□□□□□□□□□□□□□
□□□□□□□□□□□□□□□□□□

27 □□□□□□□□□□□□□□□□□□□
□□□□□□□□□□□□□□□□□□

28 □□□□□□□□□□□□□□□□□□□
□□□□□□□□□□□□□□□□□□

29 □□□□□□□□□□□□□□□□□□□
□□□□□□□□□□□□□□□□□□

30 □□□□□□□□□□□□□□□□□□□
□□□□□□□□□□□□□□□□□□

Cambridge C2 Proficiency Use of English

Test 8

For questions 1–8, read the text below and decide which answer best fits each gap. In the separate answer sheet, mark the appropriate answer (A, B, C or D).

The rise of podcasts

Back in the early 2000s, when podcasting first took off, investors didn't believe that it would be that **(1)**_____ a form of entertainment compared to what already existed in the market. How wrong they were! A quick online search for podcasts nowadays will reveal an industry that is still going **(2)**_____ and which generates vast profits. There are around 2,000 episodes released each week, covering a range of topics that would **(3)**_____ anyone's mind in terms of its diversity. So, it's clear that podcasting is **(4)**_____ and very much here to stay.

The **(5)**_____ of podcasts lies in two key areas. Firstly, they are largely inexpensive to produce, and, secondly, very little technical expertise is required to get started. And these factors mean that they are able to **(6)**_____ audiences in a way that more traditional forms of entertainment cannot. That's not to say that all podcasts have small, like-minded groups of listeners – in fact, far from it. According to recent research **(7)**_____ by a consulting company, the most popular podcasts can attract well over a million listeners.

However, professionals working in the podcast industry have issued a word of caution for those about to jump **(8)**_____ the bandwagon: Analyse what's on offer at the moment. Then, ensure that what you offer is unique enough to appeal to potential listeners scrolling through countless options on their smartphones.

1	A	tangible	B	supplementary	C	accountable	D	lucrative
2	A	strong	B	fast	C	forward	D	ahead
3	A	rush	B	split	C	alarm	D	blow
4	A	assertive	B	thriving	C	comparative	D	fertile
5	A	grace	B	beauty	C	mercy	D	dignity
6	A	signal	B	sympathise	C	target	D	imply
7	A	addressed	B	conducted	C	urged	D	instructed
8	A	on	B	to	C	in	D	with

Cambridge C2 Proficiency Use of English

For questions 9–16, read the text below and decide which word best fits each gap. Use only one word for each gap. In the separate answer sheet, write your answers in capital letters, using one box per letter.

Meeting my idol

Many people say it's not worth meeting your idol, because you've got this idealised fantasy of what they'll be like and then, in the flesh, they're nothing special, or, even worse, you discover that they've got an enormous **(9)**_____ on their shoulder. Well, this couldn't have been further from the **(10)**_____ for me and my idol experience.

I'd grown up a baseball fanatic, supporting the All Stars so obsessively that I bought all the merchandise I could lay my hands on. You **(11)**_____ it, I owned it, and I attended every game, especially to see my favourite player, Indiana Morrison, in action. I thought he was something else – the bee's knees – boy, **(12)**_____ I worship that guy!

So, **(13)**_____ I was one Saturday afternoon, shuffling along with my mom as we headed out of the mall to our station wagon, when I laid **(14)**_____ on him, 'the' Indiana Morrison, casually strolling in our direction. My mom spotted him first and was squealing beside me, urging me to approach him. My mom is a force to be reckoned **(15)**_____, and before I fathomed what was happening, and to my complete dismay, she was grabbing my sleeve and marching me in his direction. It transpired that I needn't have been so apprehensive, because he was an utterly amazing guy. Not only did he chat to us and pose for some selfies, to top it **(16)**_____ he even tossed me a signed baseball!

For questions 17–24, use the stem word on the right to form the correct word that fills each gap. In the separate answer sheet, write your answers in capital letters, using one box per letter.

Researching the family tree

The moment I ask Mary to discuss her ancestors, she begins to get misty eyed. Until recently she was unaware that she is a **(17)**_____ of a local noble family. **DESCEND**
This family was actually **(18)**_____ well- **COMPARE**
known because of their extensive charitable donations during the late 19th century. I'm composing a piece on ancestry for the local newspaper and I'm keen to know more about what drives individuals to ancestral research.

Mary is one of my interviewees and she describes a sentimental **(19)**_____ to know more about **LONG**
her roots. However, she confesses that she doesn't know why exactly. For others, the desire to investigate relatives from previous generations can be sparked by an object or property **(20)**_____ when a family member **INHERIT**
passes away.

Undertaking this research is a considerable commitment involving many hours spent laboriously scouring records of births, deaths and marriages. In order to **(21)**_____ the necessary motivation, people **SUSTAINABLE**
need to have a real interest. Sadly, many give up if the trail starts to fade in the historical record. It helps to be comfortable with **(22)**_____, too, as Mary **CERTAIN**
explains: "Whilst you hope that new evidence will complete the picture, frequently it doesn't. Records are obviously patchy and **(23)**_____ answers hard **DEFINITE**
to come by. A document can **(24)**_____ a **IMPLICATION**
connection and you get excited, but the next bit of information will refute this and you're back to square one."

For questions 25–30, complete the second sentence, using the word given, so that it has a similar meaning to the first sentence. Do not change the word provided and use between three and eight words in total. In the separate answer sheet, write your answers in capital letters, using one box per letter.

25   The rock-climbing course Jane went on enabled her to overcome her fears and try it out.

PLUCK

Jane managed to _____ go rock climbing after going on a course.

26   Borrowing money from my friends is not something I could ever feel comfortable with.

DREAM

I _____ asking my friends to help me out financially.

27   When plans go wrong in life, he just laughs and forgets all about it.

MAKE

He's able to _____ things that don't turn out as well as expected.

28   I can't think of any major problems in Philip's life so far.

NOT

Philip appears _____ any major setbacks in life.

29   When criminals go unpunished, some people think about carrying out their own form of justice.

LAW

People who feel let down by the justice system can feel like _____ own hands.

30   Although she was disappointed that she didn't get the job, it didn't take her long to accept the fact.

TERMS

After a while she _____ been offered the job.

Answer sheet: Cambridge C2 Proficiency Use of English

Test No.

Mark out of 36

Name _____ **Date** _____

Part 1: Multiple choice   8 marks

Mark the appropriate answer (A, B, C or D).

| 0 | A | **B** | C | D | |

1	A	B	C	D			5	A	B	C	D	
2	A	B	C	D			6	A	B	C	D	
3	A	B	C	D			7	A	B	C	D	
4	A	B	C	D			8	A	B	C	D	

Part 2: Open cloze   8 marks

Write your answers in capital letters, using one box per letter.

| 0 | B | E | C | A | U | S | E | | | | |

9												
10												
11												
12												
13												
14												
15												
16												

Part 3: Word formation

Write your answers in capital letters, using one box per letter.

17

18

19

20

21

22

23

24

Part 4: Key word transformation

Write your answers in capital letters, using one box per letter.

25

26

27

28

29

30

Cambridge C2 Proficiency Use of English

Test 9

For questions 1–8, read the text below and decide which answer best fits each gap. In the separate answer sheet, mark the appropriate answer (A, B, C or D).

The original child star

Child stars have had a bittersweet relationship with Hollywood. They often, through all the fame and glory, paint a sad picture of a young life dominated by **(1)**_____ parents and a troubled childhood, and this stereotype is not without foundation. There have been many children who have been thrust into the limelight and subsequently have **(2)**_____ foul of fame because their light has faded too soon or the demands of being a star were too much to take.

One child actor who escaped this rather **(3)**_____ fate was Shirley Temple, who, back in the 1930s, was **(4)**_____ as the greatest child actor of all time, and was a surefire box-office hit. However, despite being one of the most successful stars of the 1930s, by the time she was a teenager she was all but **(5)**_____ up, making films that never recaptured the popularity of her earlier work. To **(6)**_____ this off, her father had managed (or rather mismanaged) her, and she found herself with only $44 thousand of the $3 million she had made from her childhood hits.

Despite being unable to **(7)**_____ to becoming a successful adult actor, she wouldn't be **(8)**_____ off, and overcame the end of her film stardom by embracing a completely different career as a politician and US ambassador, although she apparently claimed that success in both careers came down to being a good actor!

1	**A**	pushy	**B**	dubious	**C**	superficial	**D**	shrewd
2	**A**	sunk	**B**	landed	**C**	stumbled	**D**	fallen
3	**A**	bleak	**B**	flawed	**C**	dingy	**D**	pathetic
4	**A**	cherished	**B**	saluted	**C**	hailed	**D**	glorified
5	**A**	wiped	**B**	dried	**C**	burnt	**D**	washed
6	**A**	lead	**B**	top	**C**	head	**D**	peak
7	**A**	transition	**B**	transcend	**C**	transplant	**D**	transpose
8	**A**	passed	**B**	written	**C**	called	**D**	faced

For questions 9–16, read the text below and decide which word best fits each gap. Use only one word for each gap. In the separate answer sheet, write your answers in capital letters, using one box per letter.

Thoughts from a teacher trainer

As a teacher trainer I get asked various questions on information retention, particularly whether text or video is more effective. As with most things in education, it **(9)**_____ out that the research doesn't really present a clear-cut answer. This can be troubling for many trainee teachers who are uncomfortable with uncertainty and who long **(10)**_____ something concrete to advise their students.

Our modern obsession with all things visual means that video has become a fundamental part of our lives. We use it for entertainment, on social media and as a way of informing **(11)**_____ about world events. This leads to the tempting assumption that video-based teaching is more **(12)**_____ tune with current lifestyle practices. However, while many learners report enjoying learning through video, very **(13)**_____ studies exist to suggest that this format increases knowledge retention in any meaningful way.

At this point I should mention that much of this research focuses on higher education contexts, and **(14)**_____ that I mean university settings. It may be that younger learners would retain knowledge more successfully through video than older learners would. In addition, technological advances in video-based education are coming thick and **(15)**_____. Therefore, as a trainer it is difficult to predict what new innovations lie **(16)**_____ the corner.

Whatever the case, best practice suggests that teachers should endeavour to embrace variety in the classroom wherever possible so as to cater for diverse learners.

For questions 17–24, use the stem word on the right to form the correct word that fills each gap. In the separate answer sheet, write your answers in capital letters, using one box per letter.

Wonders of Nature

The animal kingdom may give the impression of being completely different to human society, but the more that animal behaviour is observed, the more we see common characteristics. Take, for example, how zebras and wildebeests on the Serengeti form **(17)**_____ to protect themselves from more threatening animals, or **ALLY** the **(18)**_____ love shown by birds and other **CONDITION** animals towards their young.

In fact, the list of similarities between humans and other animals is extensive. For example, wolves can show **(19)**_____ by using eye contact and body **DOMINATE** language, just as humans do, with the aim to assert **(20)**_____ over others. Furthermore, in the **SUPERIOR** same way that our children play, **(21)**_____ **MATURE** animals also play, and this is a fundamental part of the learning process for all young. However, like our children, learning is often a **(22)**_____ goal, with simple **CONSCIOUS** enjoyment being the motivation for indulging in such activity.

The disposition to work hard in order to survive is also shared by humans and other animals alike. One of the most **(23)**_____ of all species is the female **INDUSTRY** Emperor Penguin, as, once they lay their eggs, they embark on a long journey back and forth to sea in order to provide food for their new-born and its father.

In fact, we can **(24)**_____ find some kind of **VARY** similarity between humans and all other animals, which might suggest that we humans aren't so extraordinary after all.

For questions 25–30, complete the second sentence, using the word given, so that it has a similar meaning to the first sentence. Do not change the word provided and use between three and eight words in total. In the separate answer sheet, write your answers in capital letters, using one box per letter.

25   Lucia denied having any involvement in the decision.

NOTHING

According to Lucia, the decision _____ her.

26   I left my sister's favourite jacket on the train and she keeps mentioning it to make me feel bad.

HARD

My sister is giving _____ for losing her jacket

27   Rescuers think that it is quite unlikely that the mountain climbers will be found.

HOLD

Rescuers don't _____ of finding the mountain climbers.

28   The problem isn't going to get any better if all you do is worry about it.

GOOD

_____ about the problem because that won't improve things.

29   To avoid having exercise on my mind all day, I make sure I do it early in the morning.

WAY

Exercising early in the morning means I can _____ and not have to worry about it.

30   In order to get things done quickly, Linda just accepts other people's approaches to doing things.

FLOW

Linda _____ to make life more efficient.

Test No.

Mark out of 36

Name _____ **Date** _____

Part 1: Multiple choice

8 marks

Mark the appropriate answer (A, B, C or D).

0	A	B	C	D

1	A	B	C	D		5	A	B	C	D
2	A	B	C	D		6	A	B	C	D
3	A	B	C	D		7	A	B	C	D
4	A	B	C	D		8	A	B	C	D

Part 2: Open cloze

8 marks

Write your answers in capital letters, using one box per letter.

0	B	E	C	A	U	S	E				

9										
10										
11										
12										
13										
14										
15										
16										

Part 3: Word formation

Write your answers in capital letters, using one box per letter.

17										
18										
19										
20										
21										
22										
23										
24										

Part 4: Key word transformation

Write your answers in capital letters, using one box per letter.

25																	
26																	
27																	
28																	
29																	
30																	

Cambridge C2 Proficiency Use of English

Test 10

For questions 1–8, read the text below and decide which answer best fits each gap. In the separate answer sheet, mark the appropriate answer (A, B, C or D).

A Race to Space

Before getting married, I was really adventurous, travelling to all sorts of faraway destinations, but, despite my exotic trips, I've always **(1)**_____ to go into space, the final frontier. Obviously, I am aware that this is a pipe dream – at $100,000 the proposed flights are completely beyond my budget. And I'm unlikely to ever find myself with the financial means for such an extravagance, **(2)**_____ a once-in-a-lifetime trip.

So, when I heard a news announcement for volunteers for a Mars project, I was beside myself with excitement, and, rather **(3)**_____ brought the subject up with my wife. Well, on reflection I ought to have **(4)**_____ the idea to myself. I'd expected her to be reluctant for me to join a space programme because of the rigorous training required, but her reaction was totally unpredictable. Rather than being fearful for my safety, she burst **(5)**_____ laughter at the thought of my application being taken seriously by the Space Agency. "Darling," she said. "I've got to **(6)**_____ it to you, your optimism is remarkable. As a somewhat overweight 50-year-old marketing manager, I'm not convinced your profile matches the essential requirements of an astronaut."

Ignoring her negative attitude, I decided to submit my application without mentioning anything more about it because she'll be **(7)**_____ the wiser if I don't get a response. However, it won't be a laughing **(8)**_____ if I get accepted!

1	**A**	dared	**B**	minded	**C**	longed	**D**	raised
2	**A**	albeit	**B**	regardless	**C**	scarcely	**D**	thereafter
3	**A**	intrepidly	**B**	unavoidably	**C**	conclusively	**D**	wholeheartedly
4	**A**	saved	**B**	held	**C**	kept	**D**	placed
5	**A**	out of	**B**	into	**C**	onto	**D**	upon
6	**A**	turn	**B**	pass	**C**	grant	**D**	hand
7	**A**	any	**B**	none	**C**	least	**D**	enough
8	**A**	matter	**B**	sense	**C**	affair	**D**	concern

For questions 9–16, read the text below and decide which word best fits each gap. Use only one word for each gap. In the separate answer sheet, write your answers in capital letters, using one box per letter.

The Mystery of the *Mary Celeste*

The mystery of the *Mary Celeste* is one that has fascinated people for hundreds of years, so much **(9)**_____ that it has given life to numerous tales and documentaries keen on theorising on or exploring its fate. The *Mary Celeste* was a large ship that was discovered set adrift in the Atlantic Ocean in November 1872, which in itself might be nothing out of the **(10)**_____, but the unique circumstances of the *Mary Celeste* are truly mystifying.

When the ship was discovered listing aimlessly at sea, the captain, his family and the entire crew were **(11)**_____ to be seen. However, **(12)**_____ made this even more curious was the fact that the ship was perfectly sea-worthy, with plenty of supplies and all its cargo intact.

Although theories abound about what might have happened to the ten people aboard the *Mary Celeste*, we still cannot ascertain the truth and perhaps we never **(13)**_____. When we scrutinise the many theories, they all seem, eventually, to be flawed. For example, if **(14)**_____ were pirates that took control of the ship, why wouldn't they seize the valuable cargo too? And what reason could there possibly be for a captain and crew to abandon a functioning ship and **(15)**_____ their chances out on the perilous ocean? The only clues we have to their fate is a missing lifeboat and a trivial leaking water pump. Nonetheless, even with this information, the answer to what happened to the *Mary Celeste* remains forever **(16)**_____ our reach.

For questions 17–24, use the stem word on the right to form the correct word that fills each gap. In the separate answer sheet, write your answers in capital letters, using one box per letter.

A musical journey

Music has always been the driving force in Nina's life. So, when aged seventeen she joined a band that needed a singer and had a weekly gig at a fancy restaurant, she was **(17)**_____ over the moon.   **DENIABLE**

The band relied on covers for their set, yet they worked tirelessly when practising to thoroughly **(18)**_____ themselves with not only the music   **FAMILIAR** and lyrics but the underlying style intended by the original artist. This they combined with a **(19)**_____   **SYSTEM** and rigorous approach to preparation. They did this to reduce the chances of any **(20)**_____   **FORESEE** disasters on stage.

Nina had been looking for likeminded musicians who believed that attention to detail could make or break any performance, so she was delighted. She found the whole relaxed approach of many bands **(21)**_____.   **BEAR**

With Nina at the helm, the band's popularity increased and they began to introduce some of their own **(22)**_____ to their set. These were lyrical   **COMPOSE** pieces influenced by their lives in a small seaside town. The songs were beautiful and audiences in the restaurant found them **(23)**_____.   **INFECT**

Gradually, as customers came to know their music, the restaurant owner requested that they ditch the covers in favour of their own songs. Within a year their set was **(24)**_____. They were composing more and   **RECOGNISE** more of their own material, and people were traveling from far and wide for an opportunity to hear them play.

Part 4   Key word transformation   Test 10

For questions 25–30, complete the second sentence, using the word given, so that it has a similar meaning to the first sentence. Do not change the word provided and use between three and eight words in total. In the separate answer sheet, write your answers in capital letters, using one box per letter.

25 I managed to do my speech at my wedding even though I was really worried.

   WENT

   Despite being nervous, I _____ my speech at my wedding.

26 Without the influence of her mother, Sonya would have chosen a career other than engineering.

   WEREN'T

   Sonya wouldn't have become an engineer _____ her mother's influence.

27 The feedback that Hari received from the theatre manager was extremely critical.

   TERMS

   The theatre manager told Hari _____ that he wasn't any good.

28 Even if they don't seem significant, try to remember as many details as you can as they could help.

   HOWEVER

   It would be good if you could remember as many details as possible, _____.

29 Although learning a new hobby is initially really hard, you should always keep going.

   HOW

   It's important to persist with a new hobby, _____ seems at first.

30 What can you recall about the moment when that man grabbed your bag?

   MIND

   _____ to that moment and tell me what you remember about the man who grabbed your bag.

Answers

Part 1: Multiple choice

1	C	fraction	5	B	flagrant
2	D	citing	6	D	donors
3	A	for	7	B	indispensable
4	D	consultation	8	C	disputes

Part 2: Open cloze

9	been	13	on
10	its	14	that
11	which	15	at
12	led	16	as

Part 3: Word formation

17	sensational	21	composition
18	expectations	22	conclusively
19	faultless	23	enthusiasts
20	omission	24	awesome

Part 4: Key word transformation

25	high time	you started looking
26	were the jury	able to return
27	prevented him	from taking part/participating
28	under no obligation	to apply/ask
29	dull as	it sounds
30	is out of the question,	as far as

Part 1: Multiple choice

1	B	sentimental	5	B	comfort
2	A	belief	6	D	hit
3	A	cast	7	A	its
4	C	remarkably	8	B	sight

Part 2: Open cloze

9	what	13	in
10	in	14	up
11	meeting	15	through
12	ease	16	play

Part 3: Word formation

17	qualifications	21	relate
18	worthy	22	resourceful
19	desirable	23	cheerfulness
20	sharpen	24	pleasurable

Part 4: Key word transformation

25	no indication	whatsoever (that)
26	lot to	contend with
27	turn their noses up	at oysters
28	is still	going strong
29	is bound	to pass
30	you hold off	(on) making any

Part 1: Multiple choice

1	B	sets	5	B	humble
2	D	element	6	C	into
3	A	gave	7	D	whom
4	D	convicted	8	A	tracked down

Part 2: Open cloze

9	as	13	a
10	what	14	it
11	others	15	their
12	of	16	up

Part 3: Word formation

17	inconceivable	21	irresistible
18	incurable	22	realisation
19	industrious	23	subconsciously
20	decaffeinated	24	characteristics

Part 4: Key word transformation

25	had it	operated on
26	would jump at	a/the chance of appearing
27	had better	not leave
28	to make	a name for
29	had to	make a run/dash for it
30	the best part	of a/the day

Part 1: Multiple choice						
1	C	treat	5	B	make
2	C	dazzling	6	A	in
3	A	end	7	A	splashing
4	D	fundamental	8	B	of

Part 2: Open cloze			
9	doubt	13	In
10	it	14	for
11	gave	15	way
12	uphill	16	take

Part 3: Word formation			
17	pursuit	21	essence
18	characteristic	22	strategically
19	likelihood	23	originate
20	consultant	24	ambiguities

Part 4: Key word transformation		
25	was on the verge	of leaving
26	will be at	the expense of
27	nothing could be	done about
28	got off on	the wrong foot
29	had got	a move
30	Only when	everybody/everyone has finished

Part 1: Multiple choice

1	B	proceeded to	5	C	innate	
2	D	bite	6	B	down	
3	A	circle	7	D	all honesty	
4	A	endowed	8	C	rule	

Part 2: Open cloze

9	it	13	from
10	got	14	of
11	little	15	as
12	with	16	a

Part 3: Word formation

17	hazardous	21	uncertainty
18	senselessly	22	indefinitely
19	unaffected	23	inexplicable
20	merciless	24	unrecognisable

Part 4: Key word transformation

25	is due to	land fifteen/15 minutes ahead
26	doesn't/does not take	kindly to people
27	had the film	started
28	to take exception	to the
29	like water off	a duck's back
30	turn her back on	somebody who/that

Part 1: Multiple choice

1	A	down	5	B	amid
2	D	legislation	6	D	ease
3	A	lenient	7	B	squarely
4	C	charges	8	A	turned

Part 2: Open cloze

9	down	13	this
10	One	14	out
11	way	15	came
12	to	16	would

Part 3: Word formation

17	unattainable	21	intellectual
18	perception	22	stimulus
19	exemplify	23	persistent
20	misinterpret	24	readily

Part 4: Key word transformation

25	faintest idea	(about) what
26	was nothing short	of a
27	did they know	that they had
28	had a great idea	up his sleeve
29	on the condition that	he wouldn't/would not/didn't/did not
30	subjected him to	hours of questioning/questions

Part 1: Multiple choice					
1	B	regime	5	D	probability
2	C	throw	6	C	incremental
3	B	feat	7	A	consistent
4	A	incorporate	8	B	the motions

Part 2: Open cloze			
9	with	13	to
10	what	14	only
11	no	15	took
12	account	16	had

Part 3: Word formation			
17	reportedly	21	justified / justifiable
18	monetary	22	thoughtless
19	confrontation	23	differentiate
20	irrational	24	unapologetic

Part 4: Key word transformation		
25	far more likely	to be
26	make	a go of
27	had it not / if it hadn't	been for
28	can/could be	posted to
29	Harry is	running the risk of
30	a change	of heart

Part 1: Multiple choice

1	D	lucrative	5	B	beauty
2	A	strong	6	C	target
3	D	blow	7	B	conducted
4	B	thriving	8	A	on

Part 2: Open cloze

9	chip	13	there
10	truth	14	eyes
11	name	15	with
12	did	16	off

Part 3: Word formation

17	descendant	21	sustain
18	comparatively	22	uncertainty
19	longing	23	definitive
20	inherited	24	imply

Part 4: Key word transformation

25	pluck up	the courage to
26	would/could not / never	dream of
27	make	light of
28	not to / to not	have had
29	taking the law	into their
30	came to terms with	not having

Part 1: Multiple choice

1	A	pushy	5	D	washed
2	D	fallen	6	B	top
3	A	bleak	7	A	transition
4	C	hailed	8	B	written

Part 2: Open cloze

9	turns	13	few
10	for	14	by
11	ourselves	15	fast
12	in	16	around

Part 3: Word formation

17	alliances	21	immature
18	unconditional	22	subconscious
19	dominance	23	industrious
20	superiority	24	invariably

Part 4: Key word transformation

25	had/was	nothing to do with
26	me	a hard time
27	hold out	much/any hope
28	It's no good	worrying
29	get it	out of the way
30	goes with	the flow

Part 1: Multiple choice					
1	C	longed	5	B	into
2	A	albeit	6	D	hand
3	A	intrepidly	7	B	none
4	C	kept	8	A	matter

Part 2: Open cloze			
9	so	13	will
10	ordinary	14	it
11	nowhere	15	take
12	what	16	beyond

Part 3: Word formation			
17	undeniably	21	unbearable
18	familiarise	22	compositions
19	systematic	23	infectious
20	unforeseen	24	unrecognisable

Part 4: Key word transformation		
25	went	through with
26	if it	weren't for
27	in no	uncertain terms
28	however insignificant	they (may/might) seem
29	no matter	how hard it
30	Cast your	mind back

Notes

Notes

Notes

Notes

Notes

Printed in the USA
CPSIA information can be obtained
at www.ICGtesting.com
LVHW062321230823
756069LV00007B/351